DARKER ENDS

'Here is a proper poet, though it is hard to see how the larger literary public (greedy for flattery of their own concerns) could be brought to recognize that. But other proper poets—how many of them are left?—will recognize one of themselves.'

(*Times Literary Supplement*)

The importance of Robert Nye's work was firmly established with the publication of his two previous collections of poems, *Juvenilia* 1 and *Juvenilia* 2, and this collection can only enhance his reputation still further. The vision of these poems is at times tender, at times terrible, but always the intensity is checked by the scrupulous strength with which it is expressed. Obviously for Robert Nye, as for all proper poets, words have a magic and ultimate meaning and these forty-two poems exhibit to the full his effortless mastery of a wide and varied vocabulary of thought and feeling.

Born in 1939, Robert Nye's first poems were published in the *London Magazine* when he was sixteen. Since then his poems have appeared in all the usual places and have been broadcast by the BBC. He has also published two works of fiction, *Doubtfire* and *Tales I Told My Mother*, several books for children—including a much-praised version of *Beowulf*—and a good deal of criticism in the form of review contributions to periodicals. He is now working on plays for stage and radio and another novel. He lives in Edinburgh, is married and has six children.

DARKER ENDS

POEMS BY

ROBERT NYE

CALDER & BOYARS · LONDON

Drafts of some of these poems first appeared in
Juvenilia 1 (1961) and *Juvenilia* 2 (1963),
published in Great Britain by Scorpion Press.

First published in Great Britain 1969 by
Calder and Boyars Ltd
18 Brewer Street London W1
© *1969 by Robert Nye*
All rights reserved
SBN 7145 0185 9 Cloth edition
SBN 7145 0186 7 Paper edition
Printed offset in Great Britain by
The Camelot Press Ltd London and Southampton

To my grandmother, Louisa Elizabeth Nye

CONTENTS

DARKER ENDS

DARKER ENDS

Here's my hand turned to shadows on the wall—
Black horse, black talking fox, black crocodile—
Quick fingers beckoning darkness from white flame,
Until my son screams, 'No! chase them away!'

Why do I scare him? Fearful of my love
I'm cruelly comforted by his warm fear,
Seeing the night made perfect on the wall
In my handwriting, if illegible,
Still full of personal beasts, and terrible.

Abjure that art—it is no true delight
To lie and turn the dark to darker ends
Because my heart's dissatisfied and cold.
To tell the truth, when he is safe asleep,
I shut my eyes and let the darkness in.

NIGHT WATCH

Watching for my son to fall asleep, I fell asleep first
And woke in a dream to watch him sleep in this world
       (of all probable worlds worst)
Where he must wake in nightmare, not born free,
And nod with one eye open, on me.

Not that I would love him for heaven's sake or, worse,
Make him immortal with a curse.
Dreaming he slept I kept him safe from harm
Who was keeping me awake, and my heart warm.

Lullabies, my jackanapes, are out of date
But to remember them it is not too late:
Sing hushabye then, however much music it take,
However I wake watching for my son to wake.

CHRISTMAS EVE

On Christmas Eve in ivory air
I drag the old moon by the hair
And trot her through the cobbled snow.

The dark is cold as calvary.
The naked stars across the black
Web of the night crawl spiderly.

Child, sleep while you can. Tomorrow
I will tell you another story.
Now ride in your dreams the mare Glory,
The stud Death, and the wild colt Sorrow.

A BAT IN A BOX

The long cold cracked and I walked in the cracks
To pay the rent for the first time in weeks
And pick our post up from the farm on the top road.

That done— 'Has your son,' said the farmer's wife,
'Ever seen a bat in a box? I have one
You could take back to show him.'

And I imagined how a bat in a box
Would beat its bloodshot wings, and comb itself
With greedy claws, and eat up flies and beetles;

And how, when hanging by the wing-hooks, it
Would sleep, long ears tucked under, as if cloaked:
And how its tameness might in fact confound me.

I did not take it, back down through snow
To the lukewarm hearth.
                              Why did I not do so?

To tell you, I would have to undo winter,
Thaw my bare heart, waste its bitterness,
Losing the wry frost with some deeper drifts.

A bat,
        in a box.
                Just think of it.

DEDICATIONS

Begrudged by the promising pencraft of my name—
On the flyleaves of books I thought were mine—
Dedicating each poem to you as if
It hoped its nine letters would be read
Into the classic authorship, and free-hearted
Of Love-until-our-names-are-both-forgotten
(In such shorthands as half-admired their remembrance)
I could not yet refuse to sign myself
Or much regret you and your books are mine
For I loved the girl who read them for her virtue
And now you have my vices and my name.

A GOLDEN KNOT

In the small hours of the needful night
I watch you comb your rainy hair
And braid it up in a golden knot.

The tortoiseshell in the ember gleam
Like glazed frost on a silver thaw
Trickles bleak with its own dewiness.

The bed—narrow, cold. A dent where we were
On the pillows. Your powder pots
And puffs make snow on the black mirror.

This is not love, the needless need
To hang myself in a golden knot.
I know, I know, but love you needfully.

STOAT

As I walked home the stoat ran round
About me with a womanish sound
Dancing neither high nor low
On an oblique and wily toe,
Eyes like blue cinders in the snow.

Those eyes so used to rat and hare
Drank mine in a star-blinded stare
Until I saw you everywhere:
Your dress that drift of smothering snow,
Your face her face, your step her slow
And rampant dancing, in and out
And up and down and round about,
Until I felt the hot flesh stir
Between my legs, but not for her.

Perch at play in a water-hole
Can be spellbound by a telegraph-pole,
Cockle the wires up in their spines.
Perhaps you have dismissed such signs
With an angry kiss?
Other signs you may not dismiss:
The salmon speared by torchlight, or this
Death-rattle rising from my throat
In dimming air to see the snow-white stoat.

ANY OTHER ENEMY

A friend of mine, unable to dream,
Half sleepily awake in the crook of my arm,
Changes her mind back to sleep, complaining 'I love you'
Who might as well love any other enemy
And would, no doubt, in wartime.

THE SAME SONG

You dream a song and I begin to sing it
In a cruel voice, and so the song is ruined
That was word-perfect in your head. In anger,
You tell me to be silent. 'Still, how strange
That you should sing the same strange song I'm dreaming.
Perhaps I hummed or drummed it? and you heard.'

No, music, I've no natural explanations.
You did not sing—but I have mocked your song
In broken accents, for my own amusement.
Never with one apt voice will strangeness tell
How sometimes we catch breath and sing together
The same strange song, knowing we need no other.

AT LAST

Dear, if one day my empty heart,
Under your cheek, forgets to start
Its life-long argument with my head—
Do not rejoice that I am dead
And need a colder, harder bed,
But say: 'At last he's found the art
To hold his tongue and lose his heart.'

FAMILIAR TERMS

You say I love you for your lies?
   But that's not true.
I love your absent-hearted eyes—
   And so do you.

You say you love me for my truth?
   But that's a lie.
You love my tongue because it's smooth—
   And so do I.

You say they love who lie this way?
   I don't agree.
They lie in love and waste away—
   And so do we.

A LOAF OF BREAD

I went to the road for food, and found
Common surprise in a loaf of bread,
Holding my breath with the breath of it
And knowing that when I breathed again
It would indeed be morning and a loaf of bread
Clean in the carton there with other
Necessary purchases
Of a son unprodigalled, trying to play father.
I had not thought I could be so astonished.

Bread! I sat under the hedge
Out of a hungry wind, and the just-baked loaf
Was matter of fact as I sank my teeth
Into its crust and nibbled, then took
Swift bites out of its good and risen wholeness.

If I'd remembered I'd have sung for joy
Just to myself and the loaf in the commonplace morning—
Joy at dismissing for ever, or the time being,
Guilt at the boy I was for standing
Outside shop windows, sly nose squashed flat
Against the pane, dreaming on galleons and castles
Of cream and pastry, marshmallow, doughnut, shortbread,
Until I thought I'd faint for want of those
Unnecessary sweets which were all I wanted.

I didn't remember till now, and now's too late.
'The birds have been eating the bread again,' you say,
Cutting the bad part out.
                              Thus satisfied—
With bread and the perfect alibi—how could I sing?

A WINTER SURPRISE

Lost is the night, and loose
The day's astonishment.
I cannot bring you back
The summer way we went.
I cannot love you now
As once I loved myself,
With such a rare wild unforgiving heart.

And yet I love you with
Most gifts the evening has,
Touching your hair, your lips
With a winter surprise
So that you speak of pain,
The child quick in your womb,
And wish the day undone, the night unknown.

AN EXCELLENT MATCH

I am your glass, and mirror everywhere
The fires you burn to see, or fear to be;
The man you wish you were, I am for you,
Reflecting who you are in what we do;
Yet I am yours too much, too perfectly—

For look, our likeness has an end, and there
Beyond the glass, deeper than your self-looking,
I rage, in blank suspicion, and half-mocking,

Completed by the knowledge I can share
Those images you give me, your reflections,
Though these shine otherwise, in false directions.

It makes no difference even when the glass
Grows dark with more than night, or streaked with day
Larger than likely. Radiance and stain
Fall on you in a cold familiar way,
Fixed in a constancy I cannot pass.
The colour black is busy here, that's plain.

ANNIVERSARY

This is the wooden wedding—
Five years marred or married.
You came of your strength,
I went of my weakness,
To a time where one said, 'I love you'—
Meaning, 'I am lost. Find me!'
And the other could not sleep in an empty bed.

Now we sleep too well together
And our separate hearts dream variously.
Such self-caressing dreams . . .
You have learned my weakness, and it suits you.
I have wasted your strength, and it chokes me.
And yet you speak of this
As an anniversary. And so it is.

We will celebrate our wooden wedding
With poems written by sentimental liars
Who found love easy, a comfortable sun
To shiver under with chill complaisance,
And not as it is—the difficult moon
Crying, 'Adore me! Adore me!' and then turning
Her naked back on mortal adoration
To go whoring after other moons, other devourers.

It is an occasion for happiness
And we are happy in our perfect ruin,
Being wooden both and hacking at each other
In the name of truth, though it be only fretwork.
Five years marred or married—
Time enough for regret perhaps
In the next five, in the happier returns,
When the heart has turned to tin.

GONE OUT

Whenever you leave the house I write a poem,
To answer you or bring your questions home?
When you are here my words belong to you,
You take my breath, not as you used to do,
But for sufficient purposes of speech.
You hang upon my language like a leech.

Yet when you've gone an hour the poem fades
And I have little left but blots and shades
Of meaning, and I mean all that I say,
Which draws me out to stand and watch the way
Through the cold valley, hoping you'll come back
To give my words the simple truth they lack.

GATHERING STICKS

Snow in the wind and pinesmoke blown back
Down the awkwardly patched-up chimneystack
On her house that's at home by the wood.
Gathering sticks in the frosty dell
I stop to watch that smoke, I know well,
Which has come from the fire of her mood.

Sticks will be chopped and new water drawn
From the spring in the side of a winter dawn
By others, that's understood,
But will they turn back with cleaner hearts
Through snow and wind to where the smoke starts,
And with better fire in their blood?
Perhaps they'll just turn, as I turn now,
Not knowing why, not caring how,
With a love that does no one much good.

AN ABSENCE OF NETTLES

I like nettles, but I took
The cold scythe for your sake
To clean the way where you would walk
And make it possible
For your foreshadowed flowers.

An evening I worked there,
And another, longer; gripping
The ancient handles with a clumsy craft,
Swinging the rusty blade about my knees,
Crouched to listen to it.

The keen heads of nettles
Lopped without pity
Were raked and carried up
To a black-hearted bonfire;
The shaven earth was ready.

I pulled up such roots
As the hands can find,
And cast away pebbles;
Weeding and watering
My own grave.

But now—no flowers have come
To fit your shadows;
The earth will not accept
The seeds you sow. And who can care for
An absence of nettles, an ungrowing place?

A MIDNIGHT CREATURE, HALF UNLOVED

In the sea's false cradle
Most desolately rocked
Or on the baffling edge of sleep
Where dreams fall fast,
There have I seen the demon
And known him with my heart
Who had been otherwise unknown,
A midnight creature, half unloved,
No more to me than you.

A TROUT

Waiting for you, I sat and watched a trout
And found some warp of comfort in the thought
That I might catch or counterfeit his style
Of silence, to and fro, a subtle fool
In the dark places of the yielding stream,
But in that deeper water where you dream.

Forgive me that I have no gentleness
To be at home with you, nor business
To know you thoroughly, and only you.
With nothing done and nothing much to do
I wait to take you coldly by the hand,
Shaken with love I cannot understand.

A LEAF BLOWN UPSTREAM

Against the stream's cruel flow
a leaf is blown
back towards the pool,
in this
the wind's wish
being stronger than the stream's,
and the leaf's lack
such
it will quite obey
the lie of its luck, this way or that,
being lost
from any tall tree rooted in the land.

And will you catch
the rebel leaf
before it is drowned or combed
to formal trash
in the too shallow bed,
take it and hold it in your thrifty hand
to press to your cheek and use
as a sentimental mark
between the pages
of your unread book,
that one day, reading this,

you almost may remember
how I came to you
much against your will,
from a tree we could not name?

NOT LOOKING

You notice I never look at you when I speak?
Perhaps you have seen in this something crooked—
A fear of meeting your eyes? You would be right
So to think, for my shame of your knowing is such
I'm frightened of your gaze clean through me
Proving my little meaning to you. Yet it is not just this.

I have a way of not looking, as you see,
Which is also part of a way of seeing.
If I do not return the long stare you offer
To search me with, and you might wish I'd learn,
It is because your presence is too sharp,
Your eyes too dear for my eyes, being poor.

I was never exactly frank, you know.
Besides, it's suitable to talk to smoky air
Knowing you near at hand, inhabiting
The corner of my eye, and half my heart.
If I looked straight at you I might say much;
Might even speak of love, which would not do.

ROPES

Watching the old man and the young man
Take ropes from round about the belly
Of the haywaggon, you said,
'See how the old man coils and curls his rope
And brings it straight to hand,
While the young man leaves his ungathered.'
I knew that you looked down on what I'd wasted
But had not care enough to take it up
And make a neatness of it for your sake.

NOT LOVE

Not love, but wishing
for even a cold day
with winter back
so you might say
my dear to frost or snow
or any old twig
suddenly gifted
with how bent a grace.

OTHER TIMES

Midsummer's liquid evenings linger even
And melt the wind in autumn, when bonfires
Burn books and bones, and lend us foreign faces.
At such a heart's November I might wish
For summer's heir to come, with his cruel kiss
Sealing the promises we could not keep.

I might—but there's no greedy winter weather
To my remembering. Our appetites
Were satisfied with spring, and cloyed by June.
If August brought us famine . . . . Well, no matter.
It serves us right that when I'd think of you
My memory comes hankering back to autumn.

The gloam rains slowly; fireworks kick with green
Attach all marigoldal to the hand.
A weasel dancing by the sallows calls
Windsor to mind, and when you went tip-toe
By the breathing statue of the Copper Horse
For bashful fear it would come down to us.

The roundabouts and swings wear canvas shrouds
In gardens our ghosts visit. A bat walks—
Hare-lip, shrill membrane, hooks—as it were you.
A bat's newfangled walk, as it were you.

Dear flackering bat, or ghost, my faithless head
Has not forgot you, though our haunts are gone.

And you have gone, but still your foolishness
Imprisoned in the semblance of midsummer
Opens that lapse of memory which is snow.
'Do not remember me for I am here
At other times,' you said. At other times
I can remember but have loved enough.

KINGFISHER

His majesty the kingfisher bird often
Stands on the snow's wrist all night long,
Unbubbling at morning the film of fire,
The big chrysalis of his blue wings.

Kingfisher, fisherking, a melting music,
He falls, a sword-bright shadow, through the dusk,
A sapphire spark, a hole in heaven, head-
long Lucifer, wanderer in new winds.

Minnows and other mercies serve the king,
Shoot down the frosty stream like spindrift stars.
My cruel flame, my lambent royal watcher,
Flickers above them, quick in the tight air.

LISTENERS

Listening silence in the glass
The listening rain against.
All in the silent house asleep,
The rain and the glass awake;
All night they listen for a noise
No one is there to make.

All in the silent house asleep,
The rain and the glass awake;
Listening silence in the glass
The listening rain against.
All night they listen for a noise
Their silence cannot break.

I'VE GOT SIXPENCE

My thumbs prick upon consequence.
Moths brush the wafers of grass
And the stippleback feels his thimble
Underwater house tremble
Where their warfare was.
In the black stream is sixpence.

Into my purse I put sixpence.
Sixpence, sixpence, sixpence, sixpence,
The piece says, and FID * DEF/
DEI * GRATIA * REGINA.
My thumbs prick upon consequence.

To pay whoever comes with no pretence
I have picked up this sixpence.
My thumbs prick upon consequence.

A MOTH

'See, there, her face behind us, on the pane
That runs with night. She watches jealously
While I undress your shadow on the ceiling.
She comes and goes between us if we nap
Too near the grate, or walk before this lamp,
Sleep-walkers leading the blind colts of sleep
For them to fill the steps we make for them.'

'Put out the light. There is no one behind us:
Only a moth who wants to die too soon.
Or let her in, and welcome, for she'll find
Fire's not so hot nor flame so flattering when
You have no choice but burning, and that's hard.
Now, sleep, and no more dreams. I'll leave my best
Shoes, heels under, to ride away nightmare.'

LET IT GO

Snow fell so quick
that snow was melt
before it lasted on the ground.
The fleering pane
of gloomy fire
turned steadfastness to water also.

SHADOWS

Seek not to be her shadow for
When night comes shadows go
Into the darkness following
Her footfalls to and fro,
Bewildered by her wandering
In the bewildering snow.

Do you suppose your silences
Will warm her shadowy heart?
Or that by lying at her feet
You'll learn her truthful art?
You might as well adore the moon
Where shadows end, and start.

SOMEWHERE

A hooping in the firs,
A looming on the weir—
The wind and the rain are also lost.

A PROPER PLACE

Outside my window
two tall witch-elms
toss their inspired
green heads in the sun
and lean together
whispering.

Trees make the world
a proper place.

ECHO

Standing outside the evening
I clap my hands
that the woods
might answer
and the low hill
send back meaning.

THE BOYS

Down in the wood the boys walk wild
hunting for badger and fox;
afraid of the dark, obeying its curse,
they kill what the dark loves.
Poet, be grateful they do not run
nor hammer yet at your door,
to drive your pen through your open eye
and follow the night to its source.

THAT'S HIS TROUBLE

There sits the boy Narcissus, or some such,
　　Kissing his outcast face, and crying for it.
Not that he need enjoy himself too much!—
　　We know he is in love, and dying for it.

THE DICTIONARY COMES

Perhaps he ate the dictionary
not for love or money
but because he was hungry?

Perhaps he drank blood
not because he dreamed of Emily Brontë
drinking his blood (which he did)
but because he was thirsty?

And now he is no longer
lean with a young man's hunger,
now all wild words are bloody
and blood and bone lack language,
what should he do—
drink verbs in Africa with Rimbaud?
make dirt his daily bread?
or say, *This hunger and this thirst
were for myself, and brought no food for truth.*

And even if he should say so
might not in dream the dictionary come
to eat him whole?
The dictionary comes.
And blood completes his self-insulting flesh.

ROUGH OLD JOKER

He can cut straight down oak, to shape it well,
Just the right point, to make each piece a stake
For a white fence to keep black cattle out;
Yet with each blow he gasps as if the blade
Bit through his bone, and he the rough old joker
Who needed shaping, straightening, made sharp
To drive, or be down-driven, in the earth.
And is there tree-love in the way his hands
Chase down cold sides, stripping the spills clean off,
Holding the finished stake up to the sun?
Or hate, perhaps, of knowing how this stood
As he has not, long in a growing wood?
In love or out, he knows his work will stand
After he has a longer stake in land.

CROWSON

He died at the proper time, on Christmas Day
As we sat down to dinner—an old man
With no friends and no vices, blindly mean
With the kind of love that goes with being clean,
His chief possessions a sour bar of soap,
A flannel which reeked of him, and a steel comb
He used to keep his dry grey hair in order
Over the face as hard and proud as a doorknob;
A sick old man, but acting out his illness,
A broken man, but whole and straight in cunning,
A man whom no one loved or liked or pitied,
Whom we had wished would die, for the work's sake.
And yet, I think, I did not wish him harm.

Well he was dead at last, on Christmas Day,
And spoiled our dinner. 'Just like him,' said Twitch,
'To go and die now, after seven months
Of not quite dying. Just like him to save
His death for the wrong time, when no one's ready.
Who wants to lay out a corpse on Christmas Day?
It would serve him right if we left him, eh?'
And I agreed (although I was dismayed
Not to feel much beyond an amateur
Distaste for death) nodding in a paper crown,
Grinning at brother Twitch across a table
Set out with crackers, beer, cheap cigarettes.

Dinner completed and our bellies full,
Half-cut we went to Crowson's room.
He lay, the oxygen mask ridiculously sucked
Into his blue mouth, fish-eyes mocking us.
Beside the neat bed, on the locker,
His watch ticked fussily; his corpse
Scarcely disturbed the counterpane's perfection,
So thin he had become in these last days.
Twitch belched. 'We'd better get him over with.'

And then Twitch bullied
That sticky carcass, punched it here and there
About the bed, about the usual business:
A bag of bones shoved rudely in death's costume.
He mocked the stale flesh, fey in this last gesture—
'A Christmas present, darling'—tying a bow
On the penis, where a knot would have done,
Flirting with the shroud
As if it were the dress of some gay girl,
Taking revenge for all the dead one's age
And ugliness, knowing he would come
To this too soon—and, most of all,
For spoiling our Christmas dinner.

This is no elegy, for I did not love you,
Crowson, old man smelling of soap and tuberculosis;

Surely, for all my wrong, I did not love you
As queer Twitch did, who used you then so cruelly.
And yet, I think, I did not wish you harm.
Am I to blame for what he did to you?
The question in its asking answers 'Yes':
For where did Twitch begin and such fear end
As made me cold, incapable of tears
Or useful rage till this? and in these words
Which cannot warm you now, nor yet avenge
The insult you did not feel in my name,
The bullying no buffet could atone,
Nor prayer nor haunting expiate.

It was my faint white heart which hit you there.
It was my greed of self deflowered you
And bruised you in your death, which you thought perfect.
To ask forgiveness were another insult—
I will ask nothing but that you forget
You ever knew me, as I would forget
The big day I was born, keeping in mind
The day you died. I am forgetting now
In hope I will remember you more clearly
And in your memory wish no harm more dearly.

AN ANSWER FOR THE OWL

I am anonymous,
yet the owl
asks *Who Who Who*.
Wind weeps in the hair
of the long firs.
They are not forsaken.

I ask no questions
in the name of love
when I cry *Who*
and try to weep.

An answer for the owl
is all I want.

NOVEMBER

the sun so low
in the sky today
a squirrel leaps over it
between two trees
making a doorway

who for

———

FISHING

At thirteen he went fishing for stars.
Either for lack of hooks or love of the strict twine
Which could be taught to shiver in the hand
He fished for them, saying he fished for crabs.

No bait gets glory. He used mussels.
After school he had searched the hard
And taken plenty when the tide was out;
Now each agape, its matter manifest,
His greed made fast with a half-Gordian knot
In a new context, and sent back to the dark
About its tacit business. He felt sure
Some star that lurked or smouldered in the net
Of stars below the surface could be caught.

Crab after crab came up, acknowledging
His wasteful magic and his innocence,
But still no star rose clinging to a shell.
Once, twice, he thought he had one, but
Only an unlucky starfish floundered, half-wound
In the sea-stained twine, mocking star-need.
Sick of ambition, cold with self-deceit,
He lost his sleight of hand, let all his gear
Ride with the tide, and sat and watched the moon.

Later he learned how not to fish too much—
Or, rather, how to fish for more than stars
With less than mussels or a singing line.
He fished for nothing. And he caught the sea.

SIGNATURE is a new series of shorter works, distinguished by the highly personal and imaginative approach of the author to his subject. It will comprise works of poetry and prose, fiction and non-fiction, and will include English and American as well as authors of other nationalities in translation. The volumes are numbered and will be published simultaneously in hardcover and paperback and will often employ typographical innovations which are appropriate to the texts.